FOR YOUTH MINISTRY

Big Differences

How to Deal With Youth of Various Ages

by Sharon Adair

ABINGDON PRESS

Nashville, Tennessee

About the Writer
Sharon Adair, a deacon in The United Methodist Church, has taught "The World of the Adolescent" for Perkins School of Theology for the youth certification process and for Perkins School of Youth Ministry. She and her husband lead human sexuality workshops to junior and senior high youth all over the United States. Sharon was a youth director for many years and has served on the Conference Staff relating to Youth Ministry.

Acknowledgments
Thanks to Brian Hardesty, Dallas, Texas; Robin Johnson, Baltimore, Maryland; Fred Winslow, Lake Dallas, Texas.

SKILLABILITIES FOR YOUTH WORKERS
Big Differences:
How to Deal With Youth of Various Ages
Volume 10

SKILLABILITIES FOR YOUTH WORKERS, Vol.10
Copyright © 1998 by Abingdon Press. All rights reserved. No part of this work may be reproduced or transmitted in any form or by any means, electronic or mechanical, including photocopying or recording, or by any information storage or retrieval system, except as may be expressly permitted by the 1976 Copyright Act or in writing by the publisher. For some material, permission to photocopy is on the page. Requests for permission should be addressed to Abingdon Press, P.O. Box 801, 201 Eighth Avenue South, Nashville, TN 37202-0801. Printed in the United States of America.

Scripture quotations in this publication, unless otherwise indicated, are from the New Revised Standard Version Bible, copyright © 1989 by the Division of Christian Education of the National Council of Churches of Christ in the United States of America. Used by permission.

ISBN 0-687-08760-0

98 99 00 01 02 03 04 05 06—10 9 8 7 6 5 4 3 2 1

EDITORIAL AND DESIGN TEAM
Editor: Crystal Zinkiewicz & John Gooch
Production Editor: Sheila K. Hewitt
Design Manager: Phillip D. Francis
Designer: Sheila K. Hewitt
Cover Design: Diana Maio
 & Phillip D. Francis

ADMINISTRATIVE TEAM
Publisher: Neil M. Alexander
Vice President: Harriett Jane Olson
Executive Editor, Teaching and Study Resources: Duane A. Ewers
Editor of Youth Resources:
 M. Steven Games

CONTENTS

	page
WHY DO THIS? Why do we need to know age-level characteristics?	4
WHAT'S THE WORD? What does the Bible say about youth?	11
AGE-LEVEL CHARACTERISTICS OF YOUTH What's special about each group?	13
WORKING WITH DIFFERENT AGES What works with each group? Hints and suggestions	36
COMBINED JUNIOR & SENIOR HIGHS 9 great ideas for combining junior and senior high youth	46
SKILLS ADULTS NEED What adults need to work with junior and senior high youth	52
SAFETY Legal issues, moral boundaries, and warning signs	58
YOUR DOUBTS "But I'm not really qualified."	64
MINI-WORKSHOP A suggested training event	66
THE BIG PICTURE How does this SkillAbility fit in? What's next? Who's there to help?	71

WHY DO THIS?

Why is it important to understand the differences in junior high and senior high youth?

So that **adults** can

- have **realistic and appropriate expectations**
- effectively **reach youth where they are**
- provide activities and studies that **meet the specific needs of each grade level**

David Elkind, author of *All Grown Up and No Place to Go*, says that youth are in the "process of becoming." Erik Erikson says that "the number one task of the teenager is to find out who they are." At its optimum this means "a sense of well-being, and feeling at home with themselves." Peter C. Scales, author of *A Portrait of Young Adolescents in the 1990s*, says that these years are often seen at the "terrible toos—too much, too little, too slow, too fast."

This book identifies **junior high youth** as those in **grades 6–8** and **senior high youth** as those in **grades 9–12**.

junior high = grades 6–8   senior high = grades 9–12

Why Do This?

Benefits to Youth

Youth struggle with difficult questions. They ask:

- Who am I?
- How am I different from others?
- How can I come to terms with my imperfections?
- How — and why — do I want to be like others?
- What is there in others I want to integrate into my life?

Youth "borrow" and "try on" values and lifestyles from others.

It takes time for them to decide which ones are a "good fit." Society cheats youth by not allowing them the time they need for differentiation and integration. Youth are pushed earlier and earlier to make decisions and take on lifestyles and values before they are ready. This immaturity can lead to unhealthy decisions.

For example:

- Many youth start dating before they are mature enough to handle situations that might arise:

    —how to say "no" when their date wants to go "too far"
    —what to do when drinking gets out of hand at a party
    —when their date has been drinking and insists on driving home.

- Youth are encouraged by advertisements to wear clothes that give the impression that the youth are older than they are so that they can attract the attention of older teens.

- Youth are given the impression that smoking and drinking are cool and that using either shows maturity.

- Youth are led to believe that everyone is involved in sexual activity.

Why Do This?

What the Church Can Do

- Provide a "youth-friendly" atmosphere where youth are given time and a safe arena to try on their values and life styles.
- Establish a clearly defined value system against which youth can test other values and discover their own.
- Set markers and rites of passage. Youth need celebrations for passages in their lives - going from junior high to high school, drivers license, braces, confirmation, graduation from high school.
- Allow an atmosphere that de-emphasizes society's values such as success, consumer products, dress, looks, money, popularity.
- Respond to the needs of the youth in frank and realistic terms.

If not, youth will find the church irrelevant and leave.

Big Differences: How to Deal With Youth of Various Ages

Assets Make a Big Difference

Search Institute has defined **40 key assets** that make a difference in the quality of life. Youth who have made a successful transition from childhood to adulthood possess these assets. Research indicates that certain assets are imperative for this transition and movement into adulthood to be a success. Among them are

YOUTH AS RESOURCES — Asset #8
Youth are given useful roles in community life.

SERVICE TO OTHERS — Asset #9
Youth gives one hour or more per week to serving in the community.

SAFETY — Asset #10
The youth feels safe in home, school, and neighborhood.

ADULT ROLE MODELS — Asset #14
Parent(s) and other adults model prosocial behavior.

CREATIVE ACTIVITIES — Asset #17
The youth is involved in three or more hours per week in lessons or practice in music, theatre, or other arts.

© 1996 Search Institute, 700 South 3rd Street, Minneapolis, MN 55415, 612-376-8955. Used by permission.

Why Do This?

YOUTH PROGRAMS — Asset #18
Young person is involved in three or more hours per week in sports, clubs, or organizations at school and/or in community organizations.

RELIGIOUS COMMUNITY — Asset #19
Young person is involved one or more hours per week.

CARING — Asset #26
Young person places high value on helping other people.

INTERPERSONAL COMPETENCE — Asset #33
Young person has empathy, sensitivity, friendship skills.

SENSE OF PURPOSE — Asset #39
Young person reports "my life has a purpose."

© 1996 Search Institute, 700 South 3rd Street, Minneapolis, MN 55415, 612-376-8955. Used by permission.

WHAT'S THE WORD?

What Does the Bible Say About Youth?

Luke 15:11–32—A younger son returns home after living a wild life and the older brother is very jealous that his father welcomes the younger son with open arms. Jesus' story teaches us about grace and God's unconditional love for us. It also has a word about sibling rivalry. **Youth often feel they are under pressure to live up to a brother or sister and may experience jealousy.**

Matthew 14:22–33—Peter tries to walk on the water to Jesus, but fails. **Youth feel pressure and a fear of failure from others' expectations.**

What's the Word?

Matthew 20:20-28—The mother of James and John wants positions of power for them. **Youth are under a great deal of pressure from parents — for places on teams, grades, awards.**

Matthew 18:1-5—The disciples argue about who is the greatest. Jesus responds that they must become like a little child in faith. **Youth at all ages have much to offer in terms of their faith.**

Luke 17:11-19—Jesus cleanses 10 lepers and only one returns to thank him. Adults who work with youth don't always feel appreciated. **Youth do not always know how to express appreciation.**

Luke 19:1-10—Jesus goes to eat with Zacchaeus, whose whole life is changed. **A ministry of relationship can change the lives of youth.**

1 Corinthians 13:11—In the context of a description of love, this verse reminds us of the difference between being a child and being an adult. **Youth are in the period of transition between childhood and adulthood; sometimes they show characteristics of both.**

Age-Level Characteristics of Youth

Youth are individuals and develop at their own pace. A teen who matures later than her or his peers may feel uncomfortable, but maturing late does not affect development toward adulthood. The descriptions here are broad, and not every individual will fit into them.

Age-Level Characteristics

PHYSICAL

When my daughter was 12, she had two posters on the wall in her room. One was a Calvin Klein ad with a man stretched on his stomach on the beach wearing only jeans. The other was the puppet "Miss Piggy."

These posters tell us something about junior high youth. They have one foot in childhood and one in adolescence. They are in transition from childhood into adolescence. Many youth mourn the loss of childhood pleasures and are fearful of their new responsibilities.

Their bodies as well as their lives are changing at an accelerated pace. Dramatic hormone changes initiate puberty, which brings a girl's first menstrual cycle and a boy's first ejaculation. Other changes in girls include breast development, pelvic changes and body hair growth. Boys develop facial and body hair, active sweat glands, voice changes and muscular definition. Junior high sexuality is linked to discovery — their own bodies and the bodies of others.

In older adolescents, a girl's physical changes have slowed down and she is more comfortable with her body. Boys may still be experiencing rapid changes, sometimes three to four years behind the girls. At age 15 or 16 the boys start to catch up. Sexuality is now tied to relationships.

> There are still feelings of inadequacy and not measuring up to others.

PARENTS

Here is a conversation between 15-year-old Jamie and her parents as she walks out the door on Friday night.

Youth are stretching the limits and the comfortable world that included their parents. Though family is still important, their world is rapidly expanding. The primary psychological task is to separate from their parents and become unique individuals.

Junior high youth have a love/hate relationship with parents and may rebel in brief pulses. They are still dependent on their parents but are trying hard not to be.

The separation is even more evident with **senior highs.** Their primary relationships shift from parents to peers. Rebellion may be less intense but more sustained. Parents lose a great deal of control once a youth walks out the door and gets behind the wheel of a car. Youth are working to establish a clearly defined identity apart from their parents and peers. This is one of the most important life tasks they will ever face.

FAITH

Youth, especially senior highs, ask tough questions. To do so is a normal and appropriate step on the way to mature faith.

"Why does God let bad things happen to good people?"

"If you have to believe in Jesus to get to heaven, does that mean that Linda, my Jewish friend, won't go to heaven?"

"I prayed that I would pass the math test, and I didn't. I thought that God answered prayers."

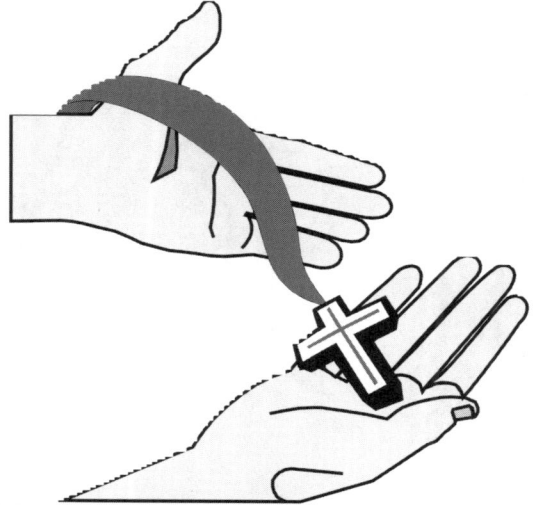

Junior high youth may see God as abstract "church" or "someone up there." God is a distant figure, but important in their lives. God is a benevolent parent. Younger youth find God in the church and through the youth g

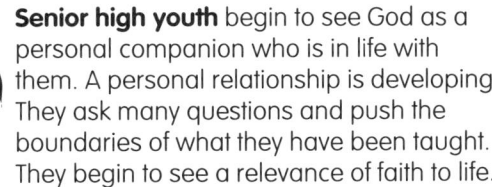

Senior high youth begin to see God as a personal companion who is in life with them. A personal relationship is developing. They ask many questions and push the boundaries of what they have been taught. They begin to see a relevance of faith to life. Church becomes a community and the body of Christ.

Age-Level Characteristics of Youth

THINKING

One day several junior high girls came to visit my office. They were kidding one of the girls about her new boyfriend. I asked the girl what he was like. She said that he had blonde hair and blue eyes and was very smart.

Later the same day, a senior high boy was in my office talking about how wonderful his girlfriend was. He said that she was always there for him and was always willing to listen to him. She liked his friends. He said that he also had good morals and that she believed that it was important to go to church.

Notice how different the descriptions were? One was very superficial. The other was more thoughtful and mature.

Junior high youth do not ask as many questions as senior high youth, and they are more ready to accept what they have been taught. Their thinking is very concrete, and they are just beginning to move to more abstract thinking. Much of their thinking is limited to direct experience. Their attention span is short.

Senior high youth are capable of more complex and abstract thoughts and asking deeper questions, especially about their faith. They enjoy dealing with ideas. They are beginning to think through consequences, although skills are limited and often flawed. Later adolescence can be a time of testing—thoughts, beliefs, boundaries. Senior high youth have a longer attention span. They are oriented to a larger world than the one immediately around them.

Age-Level Characteristics of Youth

SELF-ORIENTATION

Junior high youth are very self-oriented; so are senior high youth. A big question is

Senior high youth can more easily see themselves as part of a larger world. They may ask:

IMAGINARY AUDIENCE

One Sunday morning I missed Carolyn, president of the youth group, and someone who rarely missed church. I asked her mother if she were sick. Her mother answered, "No, her hair didn't look good so she wouldn't come."

Youth see themselves as **performers,** watched by a world that sees all their faults.

Age-Level Characteristics of Youth

PERSONAL FABLE

One of the girls in my youth group was sitting in my office sobbing. Her boyfriend had just broken up with her. She couldn't understand it because just last week he had told her how much he loved her. I started sharing a time I could remember when a similar thing happened to me. She brushed it off saying, "But you can't understand how I feel because we were more in love than anyone has even been."

Youth believe that they are the first person in history to experience what they are feeling.

EGOCENTRICISM

"I would never do that!. I can't understand why anyone would," a ninth grade girl declares during a youth program on issues.

Youth are centered on their individual point of view and are often unable to see the views of others.

Moving out from center

is a sign of growing maturity.

Age-Level Characteristics of Youth

PEERS

It is not unusual to hear parents exclaim: "She is always on the phone. That's all she does - talk, talk, talk. I can't get her to do anything else!"

Peers begin to play a more important role in the lives of **junior high youth.** Talking on the phone is part of the development of socialization skills. Peers have a great deal of influence on their social life and choice of clothing. Groups are important. Opposite sex relationships are very short term. Friends are very important and they tend to run in packs.

Senior high youth seem interested in establishing more intimate and longer relationships, especially with the opposite sex. They seek out individuals in dating and in friendships. They begin to make commitments. Failure to develop intimate relationships seriously impedes growth in self-confidence and the ability to establish stable relationships as an adult.

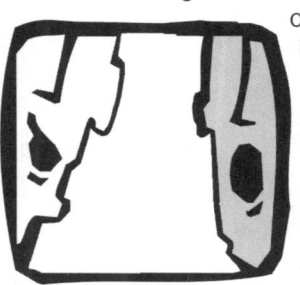

Big Differences: How to Deal With Youth of Various Ages

VERBAL SKILLS

Dad: What time do you expect to get home tonight?
Son: (Silence.)
Dad: Did you hear me? I asked you a question.
Son: (Silence.)
Dad: (Raising voice.) I asked you a question, and I want an answer now!
Son: (Hesitantly.) Maybe around 11:00.

Junior high youth are slowly developing verbal skills. They are resistant to practicing these skills for fear that they will come across to others as stupid. They are hesitant with their answers because they have so many possibilities swimming around in their heads. They may be playing out each response to see what the reaction will be. Their slowness to answer may be seen as rebellion when it is actually a weighing of the options.

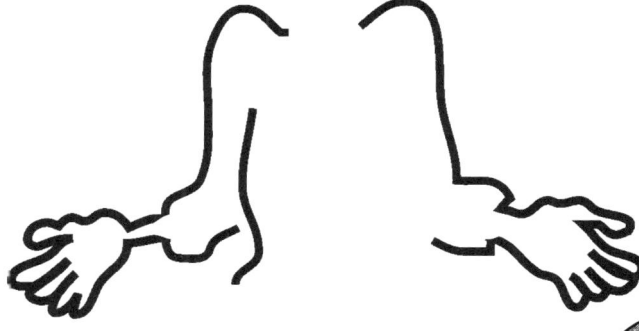

Age-Level Characteristics

Senior highs' verbal skills are improving, and much of their thinking is done verbally. This may cause problems when they "test ideas out loud." They may throw out ideas just to see how they are received by parents and other adults. They may not even begin to believe what they're saying—they just want to test it out as part of the process of developing a value system. They may say:

"There is nothing wrong with having sex before you are married if you love the person and take precautions."

"Greg's parents are really unfair. They never let him go anywhere."

"That teacher wouldn't change my grade and I was only a day late with the assignment. What a turkey!"

"I can stay out as late as I want. I won't get into any trouble. I can take care of myself."

If you can accept these statements and help youth think about the implications, you will be a great leader. If you are "shocked," you may find more wild statements thrown at you

just to get your goat.

INVINCIBLE

I once said to my youth group, "Bob and Jim were killed last weekend on that bad curve because they had been drinking and couldn't control the car. How could you go to a party the following weekend and drink?" Their response:

"It won't happen to us. We're careful."

Youth see themselves as invincible.

Bad things happen only to others. It is very difficult for youth, especially **junior high youth,** to project too far into the future. They cannot see consequences in their mind.

As they mature, **senior high youth** begin to think about their future and the impact of present decisions on this future. This includes career choices. However, behavior does not always match up with these projections. This explains much of their at-risk behavior. One way to avoid at-risk behavior is to help youth develop their ability to project into the future.

VALUES AND DECISIONS

My husband and I teach human sexuality courses. We play an intimacy timeline game, where the players place each step in a relationship on a timeline. They decide which comes first, kissing or flirting, for example. The others playing the game often try to talk a youth into moving an act up or down the scale. We encourage them to make their own decisions, but we definitely see

the strong influence of the group.

Big Differences: How to Deal With Youth of Various Ages

Junior high youth take on the values of their parents and mimic their parents' words. Decisions are clear—there is no ambiguity. But because they are unsure of their own identity, junior high youth often also follow the group mentality for many of their decisions. They may go through short bursts of rebellion against parents' values as they push the boundaries. Many junior high continue to rely on their parents or what parents have taught for decisions about values.

Senior high youth are more confident of their own identity, but still somewhat insecure. Insecurity may come across as flippancy or self-assurance. Senior high youth begin to restructure their own values, but these are often surprisingly similar to those of their parents. They may go through a period of rebellion as they sort out their own values apart from those of their parents.

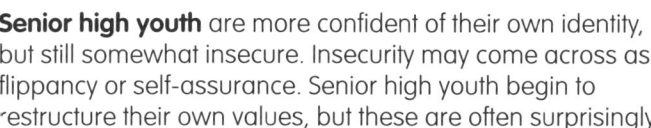

Age-Level Characteristics of Youth

Age-Level Characteristics

Junior High Youth

PHYSICAL
Their bodies, as well as their lives, are changing at an accelerated pace.

SEXUALITY
Sexuality is linked to their own body and they have curiosity about the opposite sex's body.

PARENTS
They have a love/hate relationship with parents and may rebel in brief pulses.

PEERS
Friends are very important; they tend to run in packs.

FAITH
They may see God as abstract "church" or "someone up there."

THINKING
They are just beginning to move from concrete to more abstract thinking.

Big Differences: How to Deal With Youth of Various Ages

Senior High Youth

Age-Level Characteristics

PHYSICAL
Girls' physical changes have slowed down; females are more comfortable with their body. Boys are still experiencing rapid changes.

SEXUALITY
Sexuality is tied to relationships.

PARENTS
Rebellion may be less intense but more sustained.

PEERS
They are interested in establishing longer and more intimate relationships.

FAITH
They view God as a personal companion who interacts in their life.

THINKING
They are capable of more complex and abstract thoughts and of asking deeper questions.

Junior High Youth (continued)

SELF-ORIENTED
Their big question is "Do you like me?"

VERBAL
Their verbal skills are just starting to develop. They are resistant to practicing these skills for fear that they will come across as stupid.

VALUES AND DECISIONS
They take on the values of their parents and mimic their parents' words. Their decisions are very clear cut; they have a group mentality for many of their decisions.

INVINCIBLE
They believe that bad things happen only to others.

Senior High Youth (continued)

SELF-ORIENTED
Their big question is "Do I like myself in relation to others?"

VERBAL
More of their thinking is done verbally.

VALUES AND DECISIONS
They are beginning to restructure their own values.

INVINCIBLE
They think about their future and the impact of their present decisions on this future, but their behavior does not always match.

WORKING WITH DIFFERENT AGES

1 MISSION TRIPS

Take **junior high youth** on mission trips, but plan for plenty of fun activities and shorter work days. Junior high youth lose interest after four or five hours and begin playing around rather than working. If they do work longer hours, they may accomplish very little. Time to debrief and reflect every evening is crucial. Junior high youth need to be reminded of why they are doing the work — and that it is ministry.

Senior high youth love to go on mission trips. They see a larger world than just their daily lives. Mission trips give them a sense of serving beyond themselves and an openness to worlds very different than their own.

Mission trips help develop Asset #39, Sense of Purpose, and Asset #9, Community Service—assets youth need to be successful. (See pages 9 and 10.)

2 PROGRAMS

Junior high youth need learning sessions that include both activity and discussion time. Activities/discussions need to be brief and allow for movement.

Senior high youth are ready to discuss in more depth, especially topics they feel strongly about, such as abortion, homosexuality, or faith issues. They still appreciate learning activities, but you can plan more time for discussion. Senior high youth like to know what Scripture says about topics, though they may not always agree with the Scripture.

Programs help build Asset #17, Creative Activities; and Asset #18, Youth Programs. (See page 10.)

Working With Different Ages

3 MONEY-MAKING PROJECTS

Junior high youth love projects like car washes where they can play and get dirty while they are making money. Schedule short work times to avoid boredom.

Senior high youth are more willing to work on one big project that brings in a lot of money. Too many small projects will seem like a waste of time to a senior high. Senior high youth need to know that their time is being spent in a worthwhile way. Their lives are rushed and hectic and they want to feel that the time they are giving is of value.

4 WORSHIP

Include **junior high youth** in worship planning and participation. Work with them in preparation so that they can feel "successful" about their leadership.

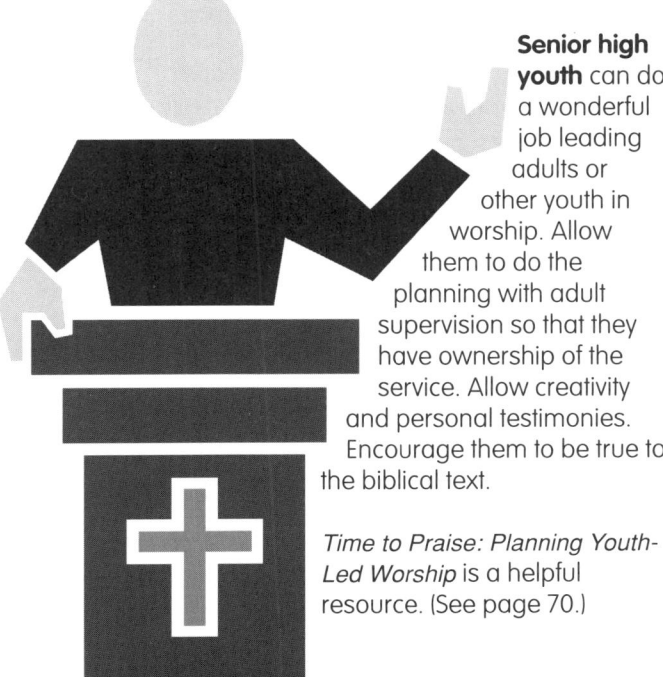

Senior high youth can do a wonderful job leading adults or other youth in worship. Allow them to do the planning with adult supervision so that they have ownership of the service. Allow creativity and personal testimonies. Encourage them to be true to the biblical text.

Time to Praise: Planning Youth-Led Worship is a helpful resource. (See page 70.)

5 RECREATION

With **junior high youth,** concentrate on group games that do not emphasize skill. Never choose for teams—there are always some youth who are not very well liked or who may lack the skills needed for the game. They are usually picked last and feel hurt. Pick teams by colors, birthdays, and so on.

Recreation for **senior high youth** is more likely to be participation in sports like volleyball and softball rather than games. Choose teams in such a way that you have both skilled and not-so-skilled players divided equally on both teams. Your athletes can shine here and perhaps exhibit leadership they could not in other settings. Sometimes this is the time a quiet youth can win acceptance. Recreation can be great for teaching inclusiveness and encouragement of those less skilled. Teams should be emphasized rather than individual skilled players.

Mudpie Olympics is a good source of non-competitive games. (See page 70.)

Big Differences: How to Deal With Youth of Various Ages

6 SINGING

Encourage some of the **junior high youth** to help lead or play guitars. Pick out songs ahead of time. You will lose the group if there is any dead time between songs. Use hand motions with the songs. Talking about the meaning of the songs is a good learning tool.

Many **senior high groups** love to sing. They are very capable of leading and playing a variety of instruments. Sometimes, even skilled singers may need an adult who can lead. Teach them how to move to the next activity by using quiet, slow songs or loud active ones depending on the activity that follows singing.

Working With Different Ages

7 SPECIAL PROJECTS

Junior high youth are great helpers, but only if given short assignments like building a backdrop for a skit to be used in worship. Be sure to praise profusely. They like to see a project finished.

Senior high youth are more willing to take on longer projects that can't be finished in one work session.

8 PRAYER

Prayer is usually an education process at the **junior high** level. Teach junior high youth to pray aloud by starting with sentence prayers and moving to longer ones. Encourage those who feel uncomfortable praying aloud to at least say one word. Help them understand that prayer is conversation and we pray like we talk. Asking for "joys and concerns" is a good way to begin or end a time together.

Senior high youth are much more open about praying aloud if they feel secure in their group. Set an accepting atmosphere and encourage them to pray. Stress more than just sentence prayers. Ask different youth to pray when the youth are together. Most youth want to be asked ahead of time to say a prayer so that they will have time to think about what they will say.

Good prayer resources are *Closer to God* and *Helping Youth Pray*. (See page 70.)

Working With Different Ages

9 ONE-DAY MISSION PROJECTS

Junior high youth love short-term mission projects. Beware of taking on on-going projects like picking up trash from the side of the road weekly. They tend to lose enthusiasm for doing the same old things.

Senior high youth seem more inclined to view the broad picture and accept on-going projects that have real value over the long haul. Beware of projects that the youth cannot see value in, such as cleaning up the yard of a home that is similar to their own.

Resources for mission projects include *All-Purpose Youth Service Kit* and *Beyond Leaf-Raking*. (See page 70.)

Big Differences: How to Deal With Youth of Various Ages

10 SHARE GROUPS

Share groups help both **junior high** and **senior high youth** deal with all that is going on in their lives. These groups must be very confidential and led by strong caring adults.

Share group issues for junior and senior high youth are very different, so they should be separate. Combining the two may stifle junior high discussion and limit the depth for senior high youth.

Share groups help develop Asset # 26, Caring; and Asset #33, Interpersonal Competence (which includes relating to other youth, listening, and helping their friends with their problems).

Combined Junior and Senior High Groups

1 HELPFUL HINTS

- Notice who does the talking during program discussions. If both junior and senior high youth talk openly, a combined group discussion is OK. If the senior high youth seem to dominate discussions, it could be that the junior high youth are intimidated.

- For most topics, the two groups do not need to be combined.

    Developmentally, they are at very different places. At least we hope that the junior high youth will not be at a point where they need to discuss peer pressure for sex on car dates.

Big Differences: How to Deal With Youth of Various Ages

- Often just the presence of senior high youth is intimidating to junior high youth. Junior high youth will usually want to meet with senior high youth because it makes them feel more mature. The older youth like to be admired and looked up to, but they also like to be in their own group.

- In reality sometimes the groups have to be combined. In these settings there can be helpful dialogue between the age levels.

- Mentoring becomes possible. Younger youth can be pushed to think about situations and their possible actions before the fact. Senior high youth help cement their own values and actions by working with younger youth.

- What ever the event, adults should set realistic goals for combined groups. With junior high youth present, senior high youth will probably not move to the kind of depth that they could if the group were strictly senior high youth.

- Whenever possible, the group should begin splitting for programs and mission trips. Most groups will grow when split into smaller age-specific groups.

Combined Junior and Senior High Groups

2 ON-SITE PROGRAMS

On-site programs are a possibility with smaller combined groups. Being on site brings a discussion to life — go to a cemetery to discuss death and resurrection or grief; go to a dump to discuss God's creation and what we do with our environment; to a boat in the water to discuss Jesus talking to the disciples and the crowds by the water or Jesus walking on the water. Smaller groups are also easier to transport than a larger group.

3 COMBINED MISSION TRIPS

There is real advantage to having all ages in work groups on a mission trip. The older youth can encourage the younger youth to stay on task. The younger youth can provide an element of play and remind the senior high that a mission trip does not have to be all work and no fun. If play is not included daily, it could be added on to the last day or two of the trip.

Big Differences: How to Deal With Youth of Various Ages

4 MENTORING

Mentoring, or matching older and younger youth, helps junior high youth with the transition into the youth group and into high school with less stress. They have at least one advocate to help them. It also helps the senior high gain an appreciation of the younger youth by getting to know them as persons and not just "those junior high brats."

5 MYSTERY TRIPS

The adventure is planned by the youth leaders and parents; youth do not know where they are going until they arrive. Mystery trips usually involve travel, going from one fun spot to another. Age does not matter on these trips. Broad age levels can even be an advantage. The older youth can help corral the younger ones. The younger youth can provide enthusiasm and energy and teach the older youth patience.

Combined Groups

6 ORIENTEERING TRIPS

Orienteering is an activity where youth are divided into groups and given directions using a compass, map, and the sun to get to a certain destination. These are usually done at a camp or outdoor setting.

7 DISCUSSION PROGRAMS

Youth programs can work in combined groups. Begin with some background or general comments by the leader. The youth then divide into age-level small groups. The leader gives the same instructions to all: "See which group can finish putting this puzzle together by working as a team." But each group works independently from the others. The follow up discussion takes part in the small group. That way each group works at its own level and depth.

8 PERFORMERS

Combined groups can enjoy Christian artists (musician, comedian, painter, and so on). You may contract with an artist and invite other churches. Some artists ask only for a love offering and others charge specific fees. They speak to youth in their own language.

9 SPEAKERS

Combined groups can enjoy the same speakers. You may ask persons in your church to talk about their careers and how they strive to be a Christian in the work place. This is a good way to involve adults who work well with youth but cannot commit to being counselors on a regular basis.

Older adults are fun to invite. They know the traditions of the church and can relate to youth in fascinating ways. It is always good after a speaker has finished to allow time for questions.

Combined Junior and Senior High Groups

SKILLS ADULTS NEED

The District Superintendent began the District Confirmation event by saying "Boys and girls..." and immediately lost his audience. At this crucial age, "boys and girls" want to be seen as emerging "youth."

1 KNOWLEDGE

Adults need to understand what youth are going through at different ages. They need knowledge of what is appropriate behavior and thinking.

Big Differences: How to Deal With Youth of Various Ages

2 DISCIPLINE

Youth group is about to begin and the junior high youth are chasing each other around the room, squealing with laughter. One of the adult leaders walks in and screams at them.

Adult leaders must be loose. Some behaviors should be overlooked. Most of the time the leaders cannot be as strict as parents or teachers. They walk a fine line between friend and adult. Leaders should have boundaries and expect some order. But an atmosphere that is too tight will turn youth away.

A good book to help adults learn how to discipline youth is *Setting Boundaries With Youth: How to Discipline With Understanding.* (See page 70.)

3 LISTENING

Sally is talking with her youth leader, Rhonda. Sally tells Rhonda that she is worried about a friend of hers in the youth group whose grades are slipping. Rhonda responds: "Grades are very important. When you let them slip, it can affect your chances of college scholarships."

Youth want an adult friend who will listen to them. Good listening skills are crucial in working with youth. Youth often ask for advice, but what they really want is for you to give them an opportunity to deal with the issue. Instead of saying, "Grades are important...," Rhonda could have said:

4 PARENTING

The youth are lining up for Sunday night snack supper. Two youth are scuffling to see who is first in line. Mary, a youth counselor, says: "Joe, behave. You are at church." (Mary is Joe's mother.)

Parents who are also counselors must allow others to parent their children when they are with the youth group. A parent is a helper in the youth group, and her own youth needs the freedom to be and equal part of the group. It is unfair when a parent singles out her own youth and gets on to him or her for behavior that is normal in the group. It is unfair when the parent takes up for her own youth in a dispute between her child and another youth. This is youth territory.

All youth should be equally free to experience both bad and good times.

5 CONFIDENTIALITY

Jack told an adult who works with the youth that his friend, Fred, went to his girl friend's house after school the day before, but had told his mother he was going to Jack's house. The youth leader immediately called Fred's mother and told her.

If youth group is to be a safe place for youth, what is said at the meeting must remain there. All persons, especially adults, must keep confidences.

Only in life-threatening situations should an adult repeat what a youth has said.

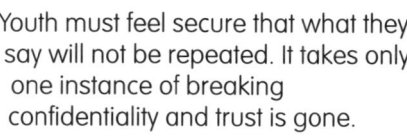

Youth must feel secure that what they say will not be repeated. It takes only one instance of breaking confidentiality and trust is gone.

Big Differences: How to Deal With Youth of Various Ages

6 MODELING

On a youth trip to an amusement park, several youth were taking turns listening to a comedian on a portable stereo. One of the counselors asked for the tape. He told the youth that, while he knew they could listen to the tape whenever they wanted, he did not approve of the degrading language or the attitude toward women this comedian had.

On his trips, they could not listen to this comedian. The counselor set a standard, and he was also using the moment to educate by stating his beliefs. Setting limits can be modeling.

Adult leaders model what faith means in everyday life. They do not have to have their faith all worked out. It is important that **they realize that they are on a journey with the youth.**

Skills Adults Need

SAFETY

YOUTH NEED PROTECTION

I once heard a youth director tell a group of adults, mostly parents, what one of the youth said in a discussion about sex. The comment was funny and everyone laughed. But I cringed with pain for the youth who was mentioned. Telling it was a terrible breach of confidentiality.

Any adult considered for working with youth should be screened very seriously. That rule applies to volunteers as well. Adults who work with youth need to belong to the church for at least six months. The other counselors or active members of the church should know them, and feel comfortable about their becoming counselors.

Never ask for volunteers. Be proactive.

Those doing the recruiting should approach candidates and explain what is expected, get responses, and then ask. Unfortunately, we are often so desperate for people to work for the youth that we will take anyone.

Screen,
  select,
    train,
      and supervise
        carefully
          the persons invited
       to work
with youth.

Safety

ADULTS NEED PROTECTION

In a law-suit-happy society, casual comments or misinterpretations of what an adult says or does can lead to trouble.

Youth are only beginning their male/female relationships and are not experienced in the subtleties involved. They may practice relationship skills on an adult leader. Doing so can be normal and healthy. The danger comes when this practicing goes too far, usually in the mind of the youth.

A very needy youth may have a crush on an adult. He or she may

- begin to hang around more than usual
- stay later than the others after events
- call to ask irrelevant questions
- leave notes
- offer to take on more responsibility than usual
- get his or her feelings hurt more often by the adult.

A youth may pick up an adult's kindness as something more than it is. A youth may see teasing as flirting. The danger to the adult comes when the youth acts on the feelings. He or she may tell parents or friends something that is untrue about the adult.

The adult must know where to draw the line.

The adult must bear the burden of the responsibility and, often, the results of the perceived relationship. It is not enough to say, "But I did not mean anything by what I did."

Camp and youth settings are difficult because they usually include hugging and affirmation. But anyone under age 18 is legally seen as the victim in most states. An adult, by virtue of age, is seen as the perpetrator.

Beware of the Pied Piper!

Some adults are themselves so needy emotionally that they encourage the attention and adoration of the youth. The relationships become unhealthy.

9 GOOD WAYS TO AVOID DANGER

1. Always have other youth or adults around you when you are talking with a youth.

2. If you are in a room alone with a youth, leave a door open so that others can see you.

3. Try to avoid getting left alone at the church with a youth. If you can't avoid this, wait outside the church for the parents to arrive (for example).

4. Avoid situations where it will be only your word against the word of a youth.

5. Try to avoid being in a car alone with a youth for long periods.

6. Don't spend too much time with one or two youth.

7. Develop friends your age and spend your free time with them.

8. Keep a record, for your own use only, of discussions that were particularly sensitive. You may need a refresher of the conversation if concerns are expressed at a later time.

9. Keep a record of complaints about you. Tell your supervisor or pastor about them immediately if you think that would be helpful for your protection.

YOUR DOUBTS

No adult I know has ever felt completely adequate working with youth. As a youth director I never had a volunteer that did not have doubts. It made me uneasy when someone wanted to work with youth because they had been a counselor for a year in another church and felt they knew what it was all about. I have been working with youth for thirty years and have never felt completely adequate. There are reasons for these feelings of inadequacy:

- Youth's lives are changing rapidly and adults cannot keep up with the music, clothes, language and interests.
- Youth want to set themselves apart from adults to establish their uniqueness.
- If adults catch on to the codes youth use, youth will rapidly change them.
- Few of us feel totally adequate in our roles as mature adults, so how can we possibly be totally adequate relating to youth? In some cases adults may do a better job working with youth than with their own families or their own lives. These are not necessarily the adults you want working with the youth.

- Adults, by virtue of the fact that they are adults, have different interests and likes.
- Many of us made mistakes as youth so we feel funny now trying to lead youth.

But grace abounds!

Just as God used people through history who were less than perfect — David, Jacob, Moses, Rahab, Rebekah, to name a few — to carry out God's plans, God can also use those of us who are less than perfect to carry out God's plans today. Adult workers with youth are not expected to be perfect. You are expected to

- admit that you are inadequate and keep trying
- work diligently on your own prayer and spiritual life
- be able to put the youth's needs ahead of your own
- continually get training that will help you improve your skills for working with youth
- attempt to help youth through these difficult transition years. Ask the youth lots of questions about themselves
- love the youth unconditionally
- listen, listen, listen
- forego lectures
- pray, laugh, and cry a lot

Mini-Workshop

This workshop could be used in a 2- to 3-hour period. Or portions of it could be used for ongoing training at monthly meetings of youth counselors. (Each adult leader needs a copy of the book.) Allow plenty of time for discussion, so your adult leaders can talk through their anxieties.

6:00 Dinner. Move to meeting area.

7:00 Prayer and Introductions-have everyone give
1. his or her name
2. what he or she does for a living
3. what age level of youth he or she works with

Ask for "popcorn" answers about why they work with youth or want to work with youth.

7:15 Allow some discussion of their doubts about being a youth leader using ideas from Chapter 9. Ask:
1. What doubts do you have?
2. What about working with youth makes you feel good?

7:30 Give a brief overview of the importance of understanding the differences between junior high youth and senior high youth, Chapter 1 including Search Institute Assets.

7:45 Briefly discuss what the Bible says using Chapter 2. Divide into groups. Have each group pick a Scripture and answer these two questions:
1. What is being said in the Scripture?
2. How does that apply to you?

8:15 Come back together as a full group. Discuss the characteristics of youth at different ages in Chapter 3. Divide into five groups. Ask each group to pick out one characteristic and do a brief skit that illustrates that characteristic. After each skit, ask:
1. Have we seen this characteristic in our youth group?
2. Without using names, give me an example.
3. After all the skits are completed ask, What have you learned about youth?

Mini-Workshop

Mini-Workshop

8:30 If your junior and senior high meet separately, review a few of the ideas for working with different ages using Chapter 4. Ask:
1. Which could be used at our church?
2. How can we use this information?
3. What have we been doing that we might need to change?
4. What have we been doing that is helpful?
5. What should we change?

8:45 If you have a combined group, go over the ideas in Chapter 5 about working with combined age groups. Ask:
1. Which would work well at our church?
2. What are some specific ideas we can use?

9:00 Go over Skills Adults Need (pages 52–57). Leaders will need to develop these skills. You may need to spend several other sessions on this. Ask:
1. Are there any you disagree with? Why?
2. Are there any you strongly agree with? Why?
3. Are there any you have doubts you can do? Why?
4. Are there any you are unsure about?

9:30 Discuss legal issues, Chapter 7. These may be ideas new workers with youth have never considered. Ask:
1. Do you have questions about any of these?
2. Have you been in any of the situations described? How did you handle the situation? How might you have handled it differently? Explain that you want them aware of possible trouble situations so they can avoid them when possible, and that you know that all situations do not fall neatly under one of the categories.

9:50 Prepare to close the session. Ask:
1. What is one thing you learned tonight?
2. Share one word that comes to mind when they think of youth.

Close with a time of prayer. Invite each person to pray aloud as he or she feels comfortable. Close prayer time.

10:00 Thank people for coming. Clean up.

Mini-Workshop

Helpful Resources

- *Five Cries of Youth*, New and Revised, Merton P. Strommen, Harper and Row
- *All Grown Up and No Place to Go*, David Elkind, Addison-Wesley Publishing Company
- *Helping Teenagers Grow Morally*, C. Ellis Nelson, Westminister/John Knox Press
- *Dancing in the Dark*, Eerdmans Publishing
- *Reviving Ophelia: Saving the Selves of Adolescent Girls*, Mary Pipher, Ballantine Books
- *The Church and the American Teenager*, Tony Campolo, Youth Specialties
- *Understanding Early Adolescence: A Framework*, John P. Hill
- *A Portrait of Young Adolescents in the 1990s*, Peter C. Scales, Search Institute, 700 South Third Street, Minneapolis, MN 55415, 1-800-888-7828
- *What Kids Need to Succeed*, Peter L. Benson, Judy Galbraith, and Pamela Espeland, Search Institute
- *Time to Praise: Planning Youth-Led Worship*, Abingdon
- *Closer to God: Youth Experiencing Prayer*, Abingdon
- *Helping Youth Pray*, SkillAbilities Series, Abingdon
- *Mudpie Olympics & 99 Other Nonedible Games*, Abingdon
- *Living in the Light: Leading Youth to Deeper Spirituality*, Abingdon
- All-Purpose Youth Service Kit, Cokesbury
- *Beyond Leaf-Raking*, Abingdon
- *Setting Boundaries With Youth*, SkillAbilities Series, Abingdon

THE BIG PICTURE

Working with youth is a little like putting together a jigsaw puzzle: It helps to have a picture of what it's supposed to look like! (See page 73.)

In effective youth ministry **vision** is central.

Seven major elements contribute to realizing that vision. The more of them that are developed and in place, the better.

Youth ministry planners in individual churches can develop each of those areas **their own way**, according to their congregation's particular resources, gifts, and priorities and the needs of their youth.

The Big Picture

How does this SkillAbility fit in this big picture? Here are just a few of the ways. By using ideas in this book, not only do you understand the big differences that age makes in understanding and ministering to and with youth, you also

- develop a **PERSPECTIVE** that recognizes the strengths of the youth at whatever stage they are and that encourages them to grow and mature.

- identify and integrate age-appropriate learning **EXPERIENCES** that better connect youth with God and God's Word

- develop a **STRUCTURE** for your youth ministry program that is inviting and comfortable for youth

- create an **ETHOS** that says "we understand who you are and how you're struggling to grow. We'll support you in that struggle and help you ask appropriate questions."

- help the **CONGREGATION** be more open to and supportive of differences in youth.

YOUTH MINISTRY: A COMPREHENSIVE APPROACH

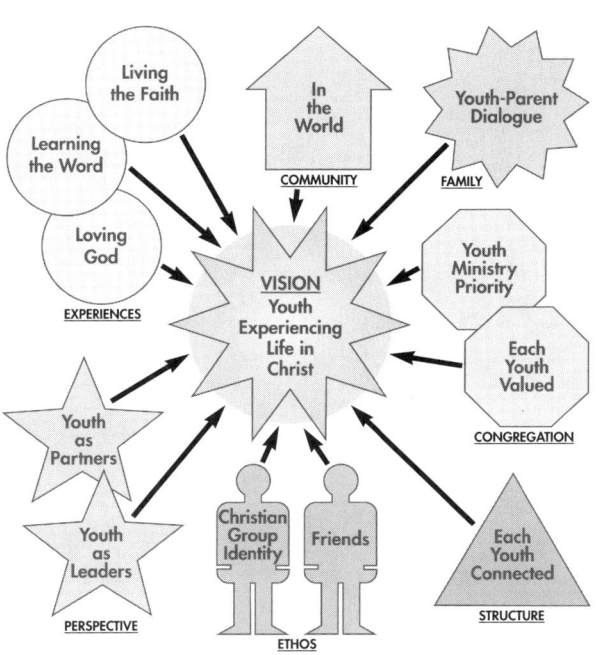

The Big Picture

The Big Picture

FAMILY

Research is clear that **parent-youth dialogue** about matters of faith is crucial for youth to develop mature faith. Youth themselves express desire to be listened to, to have boundaries, and to have parental involvement in their lives. Parents need skills for relating to their changing teens as well as assurance that their values and voice do matter to their youth. How do we in the church facilitate parent-youth dialogue?

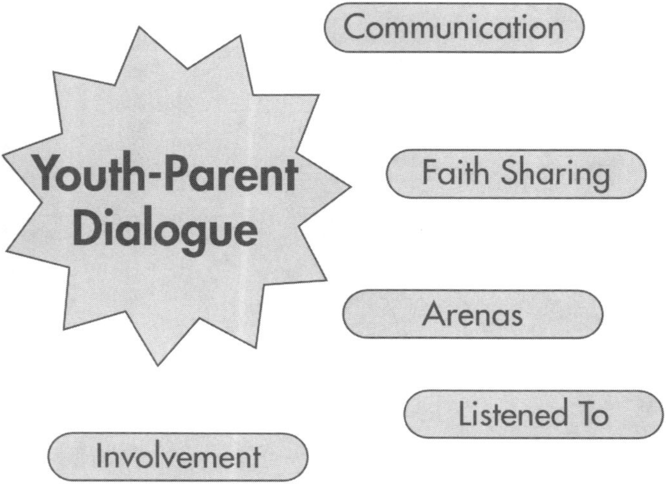

Youth-Parent Dialogue

- Communication
- Faith Sharing
- Arenas
- Listened To
- Involvement

Big Differences: How to Deal With Youth of Various Ages

CONGREGATION

Youth ministry is the ministry of the whole congregation, beginning with making **youth ministry a priority**: prayer for the ministry, people (not just one person), time, effort, training, resources, and funding. The goal for the congregation is **each youth valued**. Interaction with adults, including mentors, positive language about youth, prayer partners for each one, simply being paid attention to—these are active roles for the congregation.

Youth Ministry Priority
- Prayer
- People
- Time
- Training
- Effort

Each Youth Valued
- Funding
- Resources
- Positive Language
- Interaction With Adults
- Mentors
- Prayer

The Big Picture

The Big Picture

STRUCTURE

Whatever shape the ministry takes, the goal is to have **each youth connected**. Sunday school and youth group are only a beginning. What are the needs of the youth? What groups (even of only 2 or 3 youth) and what times would help connect young people to the faith community? How easy is it for new youth to enter? How well do we stay in touch with the changing needs of our youth? Do we have structures in place that facilitate communication? outreach? "How" can vary; it's the "why" that's crucial.

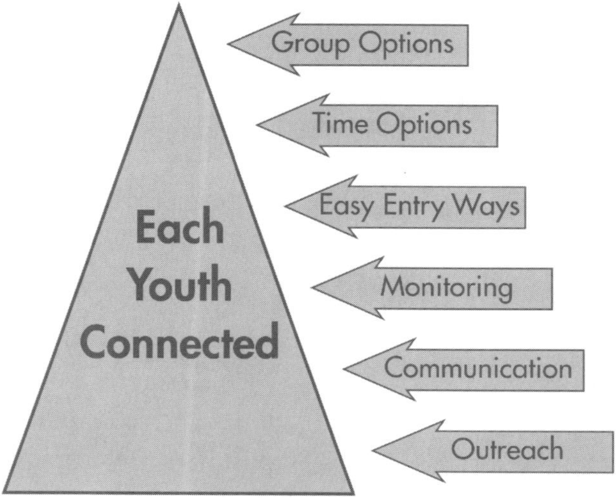

Each Youth Connected
- Group Options
- Time Options
- Easy Entry Ways
- Monitoring
- Communication
- Outreach

ETHOS

We are relational beings; we all need **friends**. The support, caring, and accountability friends provide help youth experience the love of God. As those friendships are nurtured within **Christian group identity**, young people claim for themselves a personal identity of being Christian. What language, rituals, traditions, and bonding experiences mark each grouping within the youth ministry as distinctively Christian?

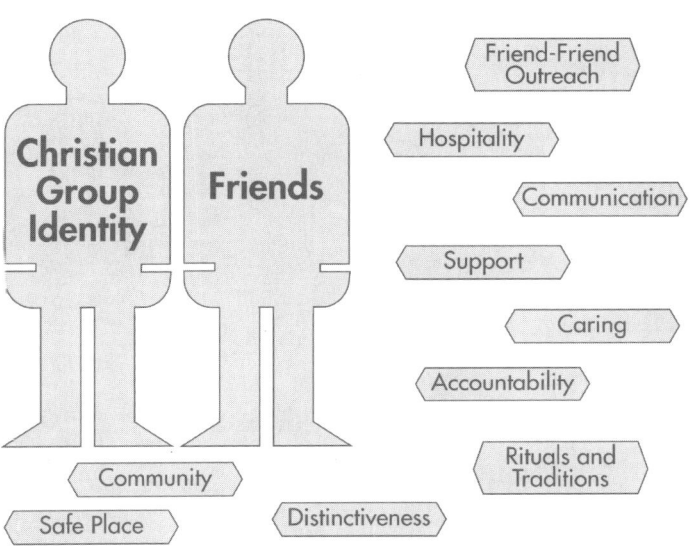

The Big Picture

PERSPECTIVE

Youth are keenly aware of being seen as problems, being treated as objects to be fixed, or as recipients too inexperienced to have anything to offer. What would happen if we operated from the perspective of seeing **youth as leaders, youth as partners**? We would listen to them more, be intentional about identifying their gifts, take seriously their input, encourage their decision making, and train them for leadership roles.

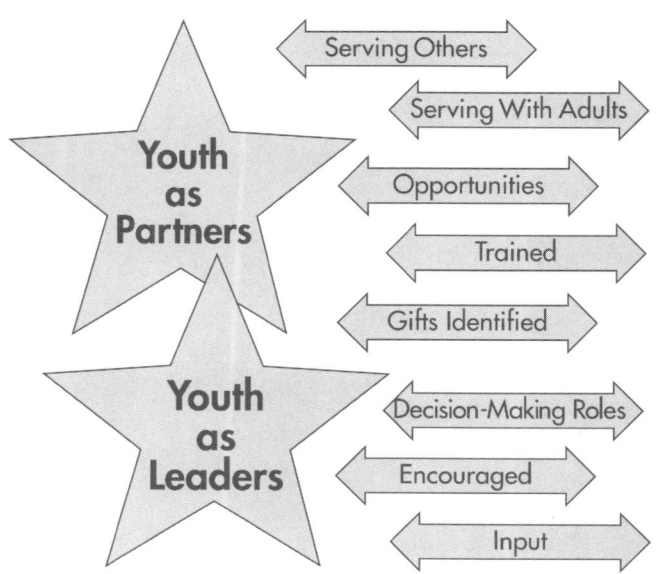

Big Differences: How to Deal With Youth of Various Ages

EXPERIENCES

Worship, devotions, prayer, and participation in the community of faith build for youth the experience of **loving God**. Study and reflection upon the Bible and the faith are crucial for **learning the Word**. Being among people who are Christian role models and grappling with difficult moral, ethical, justice, and stewardship issues help young people with **living the faith**. Curriculum resources specifically provide material to facilitate these three kinds of experiences.

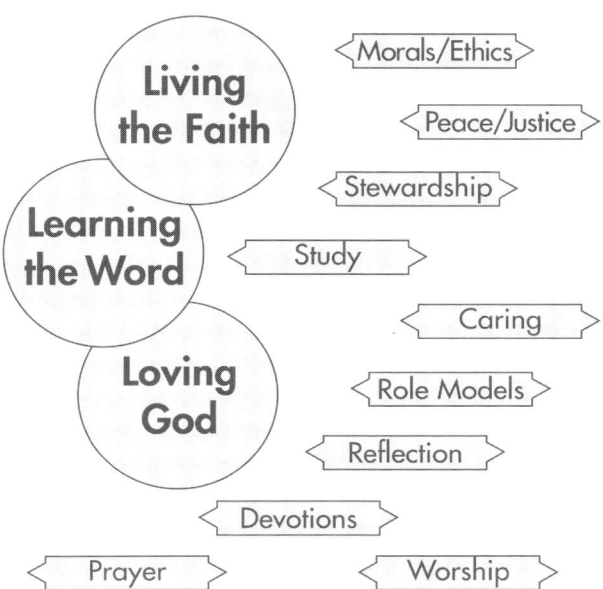

The Big Picture

The Big Picture

COMMUNITY

As Christians, youth are challenged to be **in the world** as servants, as witnesses, as leaven—making a difference with their lives, giving others a glimpse of the Kingdom. What opportunities, what training, what support do we give youth to equip them for ministry beyond the walls of the church building?

In the World

Serving

Witnessing

Leaven/Salt/Light